My World of Science

SOLIDS, LIQUIDS AND GASES

Angela Royston

Heinemann
LIBRARY

www.heinemann.co.uk/library
Visit our website to find out more information about **Heinemann Library** books.

To order:
☎ Phone 44 (0) 1865 888066
🖺 Send a fax to 44 (0) 1865 314091
💻 Visit the Heinemann Bookshop at www.heinemann.co.uk/library to browse our catalogue and order online.

First published in Great Britain by Heinemann Library, Halley Court, Jordan Hill, Oxford, OX2 8EJ, a division of Reed Educational & Professional Publishing Ltd. Heinemann is a registered trademark of Reed Educational & Professional Publishing Ltd.

OXFORD   MELBOURNE   AUCKLAND   JOHANNESBURG   BLANTYRE
GABORONE   IBADAN   PORTSMOUTH NH (USA)   CHICAGO

Designed by bigtop, Bicester, UK
Originated by Ambassador Litho Ltd.
Printed and bound in Hong Kong/China

05 04 03 02 01
10 9 8 7 6 5 4 3 2 1

ISBN 0 431 13702 1

British Library Cataloguing in Publication Data
Royston, Angela
Solids, liquids and gases. – (My world of science)
1. Matter – Properties – Juvenile literature
I. Title
530.4

Acknowledgements
The Publishers would like to thank the following for permission to reproduce photographs:
Eye Ubiquitous: p29; Pictor: p28; Robert Harding: pp5, 10, 24; Science Photo Library: John Marshall/Agstock p11; Stone: pp4, 13, 25; Trevor Clifford: pp6, 7, 8, 9, 12, 14, 15, 16, 17, 18, 19, 20, 21, 22, 23, 26; Trip: H Rogers p27.

Cover photograph reproduced with permission of Pictor.

Every effort has been made to contact copyright holders of any material reproduced in this book. Any omissions will be rectified in subsequent printings if notice is given to the Publisher.

Contents

Solids, liquids and gases 4

What is a solid? 6

Hard or soft? 8

Rough or smooth? 10

Changing shape 12

Tiny pieces 14

Liquids 16

Thick or thin? 18

Mixing solids and liquids 20

Gases 22

Air 24

Melting and freezing 26

Ice, water and steam 28

Glossary 30

Answers 31

Index 32

Any words appearing in the text in bold, **like this**, are explained in the Glossary.

Solids, liquids and gases

Everything in the world is either a solid, liquid or gas. Trees, rocks, buildings and people are solid. Rivers and lakes are liquid, and the air is a gas.

Solids are easy to touch and feel.
Liquids are runny. You usually cannot
see gases, but we know they are there.

What is a solid?

This dinosaur is a solid. A solid is something which has a definite shape. You can feel its shape when you touch it.

Each of these solids has a different shape. What shape is the ball? What shape is the book?

Hard or soft?

Some solids are hard and some are soft. This dinosaur is made of hard plastic. When you tap it, it does not change shape under your fingers.

This teddy bear is soft. When you press its fur, your fingers make a **dent**. Soft things can be nice to squeeze and cuddle.

Rough or smooth?

You can use your fingertips to feel if something is **smooth** or **rough**. The metal frame of the bicycle is so smooth that it is shiny.

The leaves of this tree are smooth, but the apples are smoother. The branches of the tree are rough – much rougher than the leaves.

Changing shape

Some things change shape easily. You can make many different shapes from modelling clay. Try stretching it and squashing it.

Some things can be bent into a different shape. A rope is so bendy it can be twisted and tied into a knot. The branch of the tree can bend too.

Tiny pieces

Some solids are broken up into tiny pieces. Talcum powder, flour and salt are sold in tiny pieces because they are easier to use like that.

Solids in tiny pieces are often called powders. They can be poured from one **container** to another. They can also be poured into a **heap**.

Liquids

Liquids can be poured from one **container** to another too, but not into a **heap**. Water is the most common liquid, but there are many other liquids.

A liquid takes the shape of its container. When you pour juice from a carton into a glass, it becomes a different shape. What happens when the juice spills?

Thick or thin?

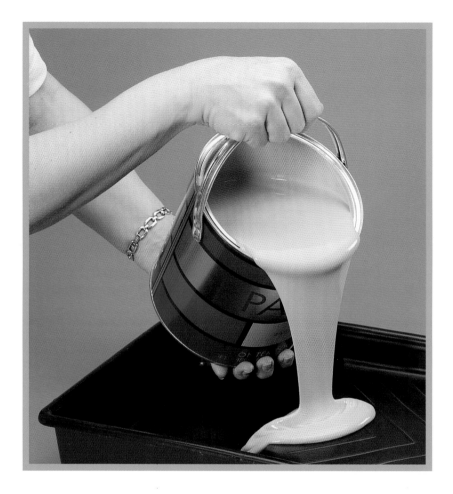

Some liquids are so thick that they can hardly be poured at all. The paint in this tin is very thick. It **flows** very slowly.

Thin liquids flow much quicker. Custard is thinner than yoghurt and flows faster than it. But custard flows slower than milk or water.

Mixing solids and liquids

Some solids and liquids can be mixed together. When you add some powdered paint to water, the water goes cloudy.

When you add salt to water, the salt seems to disappear! In fact the salt has **dissolved**. You can tell the salt is still there by tasting the water.

Gases

A gas has no particular shape. It floats
and spreads out to fill the space it is in.
The space in the bottle above the liquid
perfume is filled with perfume gas.

You cannot usually see or feel a gas.
When you open the bottle of perfume,
the gas moves out of the bottle. That is
why you can then smell it!

Air

The air is a gas. You cannot see it, but it is all around you. You can feel the air blowing on a windy day. The air is a mixture of gases.

One of the gases in the air is oxygen.
People, horses and all living things
breathe in oxygen. We all need
oxygen to stay alive.

Melting and freezing

When solids are heated, they **melt** and change into a liquid. Chocolate is usually solid, but it melts when it is heated and becomes liquid and runny.

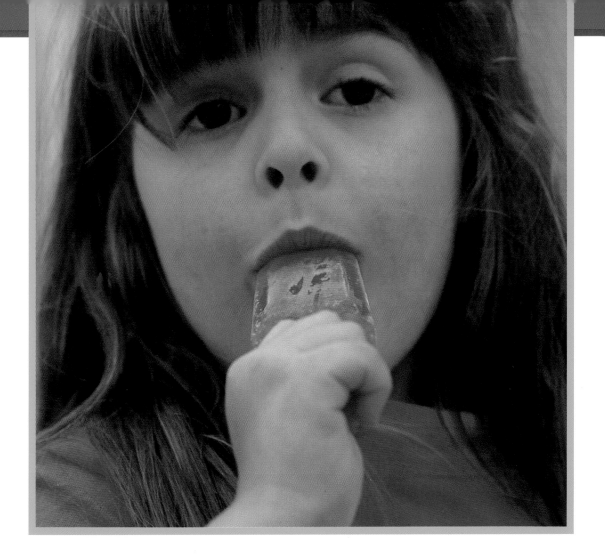

When liquids become cold enough, they
freeze and change into a solid. This ice
lolly was made by freezing liquid fruit
juice. It melts as it becomes warm.

Ice, water and steam

Water usually exists as a liquid, but it can be a solid or a gas too. When water **freezes**, it changes to solid ice. What is happening to these icicles?

When water is heated, it begins to boil.
Bubbles of gas form in the hot water.
The gas floats into the air and forms
very hot steam.

Glossary

breathe to take in and give out air

container something that you can put things in – for example, a box or jar

dent a slight mark in a solid

dissolve to mix together and disappear in a liquid

flow to move smoothly

freeze when a liquid gets very cold and becomes solid

heap a pile

melt when a solid gets warmer and becomes a liquid

rough bumpy or uneven

smooth something with an even surface

Answers

Page 7 – What is a solid?
The ball is round. The book is flat
and square.

Page 17 – Liquids
When the juice spills, it spreads out to form
a shallow puddle.

Page 28 – Ice, water and steam
The icicles are melting.

Index

air 4, 24–25, 29
chocolate 26
freezing 27, 28
gases 4–5, 22–25, 28–29
icicles 28
juice 17, 27
liquids 4–5, 16–19, 20, 22, 28
melting 26–27
oxygen 25
paint 18, 20
powder 14–15, 20
salt 14, 21
solids 4–5, 6–7, 8, 14–15, 20, 26–27, 28
steam 29
trees 4, 11, 13
water 16, 19, 20, 21, 28–29

Titles in the *My World of Science* series include:

Hardback   0 431 13713 7

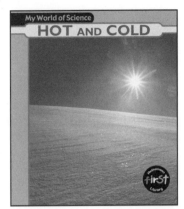

Hardback   0 431 13715 3

Hardback   0 431 13712 9

Hardback   0 431 13714 5

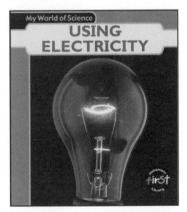

Hardback   0 431 13716 1

Find out about the other titles in this series on our website www.heinemann.co.uk/library